SPECTRUM®
READERS

LEVEL 2

EXOTIC!
Places

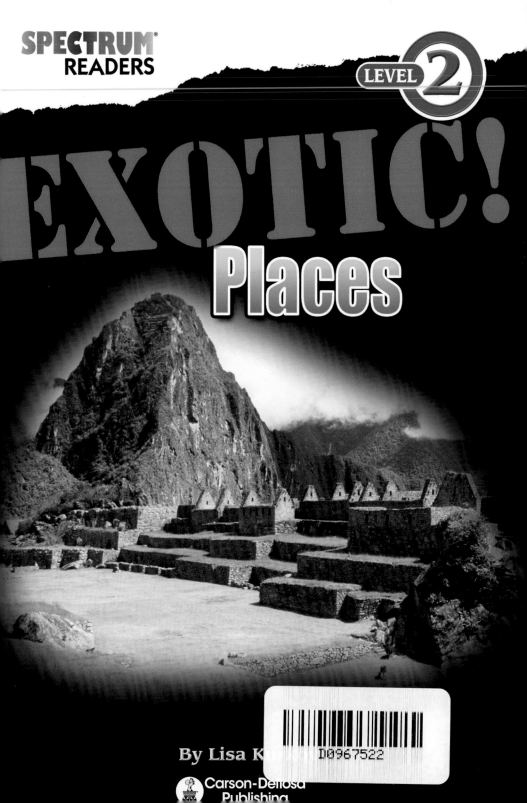

By Lisa K...

Carson-Dellosa
Publishing

SPECTRUM®

An imprint of Carson-Dellosa Publishing, LLC
P.O. Box 35665
Greensboro, NC 27425-5665

carsondellosa.com

Printed in the USA. All rights reserved.
ISBN 978-1-4838-0125-4

01-002141120

The world is full of exotic places. *Exotic* means "different or unusual." Some places are beautiful or strange. Some places are remote or mysterious. What exotic place would you most like to visit?

Bodie Ghost Town

Let's travel to California.
We can visit Bodie, a ghost town.
Thousands of people once lived here.
They came to look for gold.
The buildings still stand.
Even tables and chairs remain.
But, the town is empty.

Yellowstone Park

Let's travel to Wyoming.
We can visit Yellowstone Park.
Old Faithful is a famous geyser here.
Every 90 minutes or so, it shoots steam
and water into the air.
Watch out—the water is boiling!
The park has 300 other geysers, too.

Devil's Golf Course

Let's travel back to California.
We can visit Devil's Golf Course.
Its name is a joke.
It is too bumpy to play golf here!
A lake once covered this place.
It left behind salt and minerals,
making the land bumpy.

Machu Picchu

Let's travel to Peru.
We can visit Machu Picchu.
It is an ancient city in the mountains.
The Incas lived here 500 years ago.
The city was built with no iron, no steel, and no wheels.
How it was built is a mystery.

Antarctica

Let's travel to the South Pole.
We can visit the icy continent
of Antarctica.
Penguins live here all year long,
but people do not.
Antarctica is the coldest, windiest, and
driest place on Earth.

Cliffs of Moher

Let's travel to Ireland.
We can visit the Cliffs of Moher.
The cliffs tower over the Atlantic Ocean
for more than five miles.
Wind erodes the rocks, forming
strange shapes.
The crashing waves carve sea caves
under the cliffs.

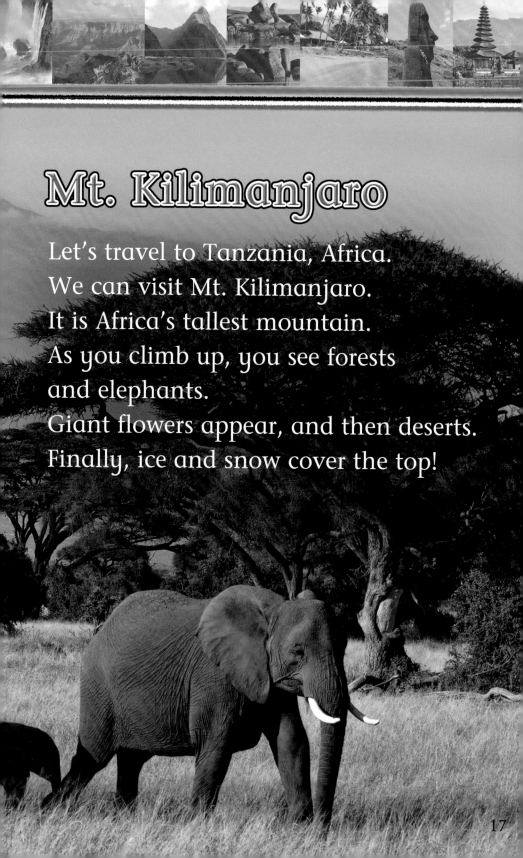

Mt. Kilimanjaro

Let's travel to Tanzania, Africa.
We can visit Mt. Kilimanjaro.
It is Africa's tallest mountain.
As you climb up, you see forests
and elephants.
Giant flowers appear, and then deserts.
Finally, ice and snow cover the top!

Victoria Falls

Let's travel to Zambia, Africa.
We can visit Victoria Falls.
These waterfalls are some of the world's
largest and most beautiful.
They lie between Zambia and Zimbabwe.
You can see the spray 30 miles away!
This place is famous for its rainbows.

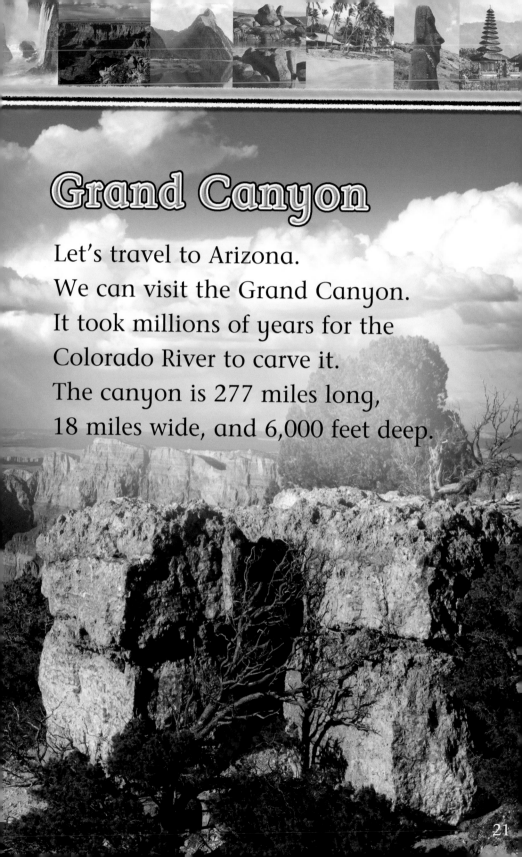

Grand Canyon

Let's travel to Arizona.
We can visit the Grand Canyon.
It took millions of years for the
Colorado River to carve it.
The canyon is 277 miles long,
18 miles wide, and 6,000 feet deep.

Milford Sound

Let's travel to New Zealand.
We can visit Milford Sound.
It has cliffs, mountains, and waterfalls.
The water is home to lots of wildlife.
You might see dolphins or penguins.
Sea stars with 11 arms live here!

Bay of Fires

Let's travel to the island of Tasmania.
We can visit the Bay of Fires.
A sea captain named the bay after he
saw the beach fires of native people.
Orange fungus covers the rocks here.
Kangaroos and Tasmanian devils live
nearby.

Fiji

Let's travel to the South Pacific Ocean.
We can visit Fiji.
The nation of Fiji is made up of more
than 300 islands.
A group of islands is called an
archipelago.
Here, you can play on tropical beaches
and explore coral reefs.

Easter Island

Let's travel farther east out into the
Pacific Ocean.
We can visit Easter Island.
Almost 900 statues stand here.
The Rapa Nui people carved these
giants 700 years ago.
A single stone statue weighs 14 tons.
That's as much as a school bus!

Bali

Let's travel to Indonesia.
We can visit the island of Bali.
Bali is covered with mountains.
Some beaches have black sand made
from volcanic rock.
Tigers live in rain forests here.
Many temples are built near lakes and
rivers.

EXOTIC! Places
Comprehension Questions

1. Why did people first come to Bodie, California?

2. About how often does Old Faithful erupt?

3. Why is the name *Devil's Golf Course* a joke?

4. What group of people lived in ancient Machu Picchu?

5. Where is Antarctica?

6. What is the name of Africa's highest mountain?

7. What is an archipelago?

8. What kinds of wildlife can you see near Milford Sound?

9. Why are the rocks in the Bay of Fires orange?